THREE CHRISTMAS JOURNEYS

Ro Willoughby

illustrated by David Miller

Abingdon Press

To Robert, Mark and Louisa as we journey together. RW
To Nancy, my first love, my mother. DM

© text 1999 Ro Willoughby
© illustrations 1999 David Miller
First published in 1999 by
Scripture Union, 207–209 Queensway, Bletchley, Milton Keynes MK2 2EB, England

Published in the United States of America by
Abingdon Press
201 Eighth Avenue South
P. O. Box 801
Nashville, TN 37202-0801

ISBN 0-687-03482-5

All rights reserved. No part of this publication may be reproduced, stored in a retrieval system, or transmitted, in any form or by any means, electronic, mechanical, photocopying, recording or otherwise, without the prior permission of Scripture Union.

The right of Ro Willoughby to be identified as author of this work has been asserted by her in accordance with the Copyright, Designs and Patents Act 1988.

British Library Cataloguing-in-Publication Data
A catalogue record of this book is available from the British Library.

Printed in Singapore by Tien Wah Press

Joseph and Mary's journey

All children dream about being grown-up. Mary was no different. She dreamed about becoming the wife of Joseph the carpenter. She dreamed about her home with wooden furniture carefully made by Joseph. She never thought she would be famous. She never dreamed about going on a long journey.

All that changed the day the angel came.

Mary was on her own at home when someone else came into the room. She looked up. Someone was standing by the door. He looked like a man and yet he seemed different.

"Mary, you will have a son," he said. "God himself will be his father. You will call him Jesus. He will be king for ever."

Mary was happy and scared all at the same time. But when she told Joseph, he was not happy at all. An angel later told him everything would be all right.

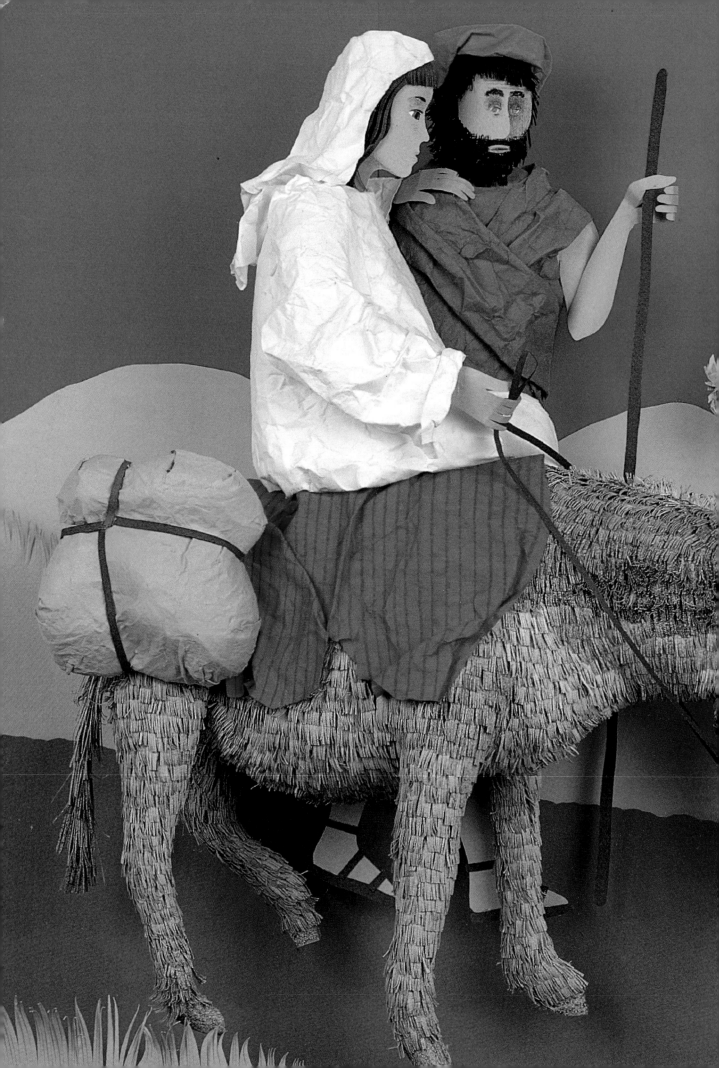

A few months later they went on a long journey.
Mary had to ride on a donkey because it was nearly
time for her baby to be born.

Joseph and Mary were not the only ones who had to make a long journey. Their land was ruled by the Romans who wanted to know the names of everyone who lived there. Everyone was ordered to go back to the place where their family came from. That's why Joseph had to go all the way to Bethlehem. He had to take his wife with him. It was a long, long journey and took them many days.

Mary was very tired when they got to Bethlehem.

"Joseph," she whispered, "I think my baby will soon be born. We need somewhere to rest. I must lie down."

Joseph asked for a room at the first guest house they came to.

"Sorry," the woman said. "We're full up."

And at the next place...

"No room here. Try next door."

And next door, the man in charge told Joseph...

"Sorry. We can't help you. Everyone has come to give their name to the Romans."

Joseph's face fell. What could he do? The man saw his face. He saw Mary, sitting bent over on the donkey. He felt sorry for them.

"Look," he said, "my animals are in the shed round the back. You can sleep there if you like. It will be warm and dry and your wife can lie down in the hay."

Gratefully Joseph took Mary to the shed. Mary lay down on the hay. The man had been right. It was warm and dry.

A few hours later, the baby was born. He let out a loud cry. Mary lay on the hay, holding him in her arms. This was her baby! This baby was God's son!

Joseph gently wrapped Jesus up and put him in the box where the hay was kept for the animals. Then they all fell asleep.

But on the hills, outside the town, some shepherds were wide awake. The fire was keeping them warm. It was a cold, cold night. The sheep stayed close by as well.

Suddenly, it was as though a spark from the fire had
exploded. There was light all around, a bright,
dazzling light which filled the sky.

The shepherds' journey

The shepherds were scared stiff. These were strong brave men who could kill a wolf or a bear. But they had seen nothing like this.

In the middle of the light there was an angel. He had a message for them from God.

"Don't be afraid," he called out. "I've got some great news for you. During the night, down below in the town, a baby has been born. He is a very important baby. He has come from God to save all people. You must go to find him."

The shepherds stared at each other. What was all this?
What did it mean? Then the angel was joined by
thousands and thousands of other angels. You couldn't
count them. And they sang so loudly and so beautifully
that the shepherds' ears nearly burst. They were
praising God over and over again.

Slowly the singing went quiet. Slowly the light
faded. The glow from the fire was the only light left.
The shepherds sat still. Then one of them jumped up.

"Come on," he said. "This is something we mustn't
miss."

So all the shepherds made their journey down the
hill into the town. They didn't go slowly like Mary's
donkey. They ran just as fast as they could.

In Bethlehem, they found the shed where Joseph
and Mary were resting. And they found the baby too!

The shepherds wanted to know what was going on.

"Who are you?" they asked Mary.

"What can you tell us about this baby?"

"Why is he so special?"

He looked just like any other baby!

Joseph told them all he could.

At last the shepherds had to go. They made their journey all the way back up the hill. They could not stop talking.

"Did you see how happy his mother was?" one of them said.

"He didn't look important but he must be if an angel said so."

"Wait until I tell my wife!"

It was all so exciting!

The wise men's journey

Far away in the East, some more men were getting ready to make a journey. They were very clever men who read many books and used very big words. They studied the sky at night to see how the stars moved.

One night, they saw a bright star, much brighter than any other star. Each night it moved a little further across the sky.

"Look at that star!" they said to each other. "What does it mean?"

They looked in their big books and at last discovered that this star meant a king had been born.

"Let's go and follow the star. Then we shall find out about this king."

Their servants took many weeks getting ready. They needed food for the journey. They knew they would have to go into another country and might be away from home for a long time. They had to take the strongest camels they could find. They also had to decide what special presents to give to the king when they found him.

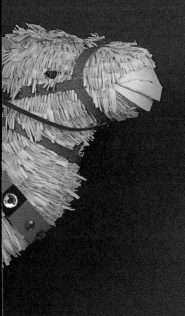

All this time, the star was slowly moving away from them across the sky.

At last everything was ready. They were off on the greatest journey they were ever to make!

The star kept moving so the camels kept going. They slept during the day. Sometimes the men rested for several days to give the camels a break.

At last they saw a large city ahead of them. This was Jerusalem, where King Herod lived. The star seemed to stop. These clever men went straight to the palace.

"The baby king must live here," they said.

King Herod was glad to see these important wise men who had traveled such a long way to see him.

They asked him, "Where is the baby king? Can we see him?"

But King Herod could not answer their questions. And no one else in the city could. King Herod became angry. Who was this king they talked about? He didn't like the sound of it at all.

The men went outside to look at the star. It was still moving! They must continue their journey.

"Come back and tell me when you have found this king," King Herod told them. "I would be most interested to see him for myself."

The camels moved steadily for one night. They came into Bethlehem, where Mary and Joseph now lived. The star had stopped over their house.

"I didn't expect a king to live in a town as small as this," one of the men said.

"And I didn't expect a king to live in a house as small as this," another one said.

"I didn't expect to give such a rich gift to anyone living in such a poor place," a third man said, as his servant gave him the present he had brought.

But once they had gone into the house, they knew the star had brought them to the right place.

These men, who were so clever and knew so much, knelt down in front of Jesus. This child was greater than they were. He truly was a king.

They gave him the presents they had brought with them.

Gold was used for a king's crown, so they gave him gold...because he was a king.

Frankincense was used when people worshipped God, so they gave him frankincense...because he was God.

Myrrh was a perfume used when a person died, so they gave him myrrh...because he was going to suffer.

Joseph and Mary tried to answer the many questions these wise men asked. At last it was time for them to leave. They had to make their journey back home. King Herod had asked them to call in on their way home. But in a dream they were warned not to go back to Jerusalem. So they went home another way.

Joseph and Mary's journey

Mary and Joseph had not finished their journey. An angel came to Joseph in a dream. He warned Joseph that Jesus was in danger. So they packed up and travelled further south, away from Jerusalem, further away from their home, all the way to Egypt.

It was some time before it was safe for them to make the journey back home.